"God has kicked off an amazing year of women's ministry! My team and I are beginning Sue Edwards's Bible study this evening, and God has touched the hearts of sixty women to be part of it—we prayed for forty. Isn't He amazing? I couldn't be more excited about working where God is at work."

—Robin Neff
Fort Wayne, Indiana

"I have confidence when I dig into a study prepared by Sue Edwards that it will be solidly based on God's Word and will speak to me uniquely as a woman. Sue takes God's timeless truth and makes it relevant to me in ways that help me know my God better and love Him more as I live out my life with a feminine heart and mind. I always look forward to her next study!"

—Clarice Clayton
Arlington, Texas

"*Daddy's Girls* enabled me to identify ways in which my relationship with my earthly father impacted my understanding of God. Through what I learned, I was then able to use the study to help other women more fully embrace and enjoy the love and acceptance of their heavenly Father."

—Dr. Joye Baker
Adjunct Professor of Christian Education
Dallas Theological Seminary

"What an incredible year we have had using Sue's curriculum. Thank you so much for the great blessing it has been to us and to all of our women. The ladies particularly loved *Daddy's Girls*. They felt it was challenging and well written."

—Phyllis Bennett
Director of Women's Ministries
Grace Baptist Church
Hudson, Massachusetts

Daddy's Girls

A SUE EDWARDS INDUCTIVE BIBLE STUDY

Daddy's Girls

DISCOVER THE WONDER OF THE FATHER

LEADER'S GUIDE INCLUDED

SUE EDWARDS

Kregel
Publications

Daddy's Girls: Discover the Wonder of the Father

© 2007 by Sue Edwards

Published by Kregel Publications, a division of Kregel, Inc., P.O. Box 2607, Grand Rapids, MI 49501.

Library of Congress Cataloging-in-Publication Data
Edwards, Sue.
   Daddy's girls : discover the wonder of the Father / by Sue Edwards.
       p.   cm.
   Includes bibliographical references.
   1. God (Christianity)—Fatherhood—Textbooks.
2. God—Worship and love—Textbooks. 3. Christian women—Religious life—Textbooks. I. Title.
BT153.F3E39   2007   231'.1—dc22   2007017202
                                                  CIP

ISBN 978-0-8254-2546-2

Printed in the United States of America

07 08 09 10 11 / 5 4 3 2 1

To my granddaughter,
Rebecca Anne Crook.
May you grow up to be a Daddy's Girl,
discovering the incredible wonder of the Father
and the joy of serving Him for a lifetime.

Contents

Acknowledgments

A special thanks to Victoria Secunda, author of *Women and Their Fathers*, and Random House/ Delacorte Press (New York, 1992) for their kind permission to use women's quotes collected in Secunda's research. To Kelley Mathews and Tina Schieferstein for their editing expertise, and Joye Baker for her friendship and support. I'm also grateful to Dennis Hillman, Steve Barclift, and Amy Stephansen (Kregel Publications) for their professionalism and integrity. And to my husband, David: thank you for your steadfast faith and gentle strength, especially in the lives of our daughters and granddaughter. You make loving God the Father natural for them—a precious gift.

How to Use This Study Guide

Women today need Bible study to keep balanced, focused, and Christ-centered in their busy worlds. The study questions in this guide allow you to choose the study level that fits your lifestyle. To provide even more flexibility, you may pick a different level each week, depending on your schedule.

- The "core" questions (designated by 1, 2, 3, etc.) require a total of about an hour-and-a-half of weekly study time, yet provide a basic understanding of the text. For busy women, this level offers in-depth Bible study with a minimum time commitment.

- The "Digging Deeper" questions require outside resources such as an atlas, Bible dictionary, and concordance. This level will challenge you to learn more about the history, culture, and geography related to the Bible. You will also be looking up parallel passages for additional insight.

- The "Summit" questions are for those who want to probe the text even more deeply. These questions grapple with complex theological issues and differing views. You're encouraged to investigate deeper by using an interlinear Greek-English text and *Vine's Expository Dictionary* on your own. Also you may create outlines, charts, and essays in seminary-style open-ended assignments. Some with teaching gifts and an interest in advanced academics will enjoy exploring the "summit."

Choose a realistic level of Bible study—one you can stick with. You may want to finish the "core" level first, and then tackle the other levels as time permits. Take time to savor the questions, and don't rush through the application. The key is consistency. Do not allow yourself to be intimidated by women who have more time or who are gifted differently from you.

Make your Bible study—whatever level you choose—top priority. Consider spacing your study throughout the week so that you can take time to ponder and meditate on what the Holy Spirit is teaching you. Do not make other appointments during the group Bible study. Ask God to enable you to attend faithfully. Come with an excitement to learn from others and a desire to share yourself and your journey. Give it your best, and God promises to join you on this adventure that can change your life.

Within the Transcendent God Beats a Father's Heart

> For most women, fathers are mystery men, constellations of piecemeal memories: Dad at work, Dad behind the newspaper, Dad fixing the car—or Dad who one day left home and never looked back.
>
> —Victoria Secunda[1]

The first men in our lives affect us in profound ways—having an impact on our relationships with men every day as well as our relationship with our heavenly Father. You may have had a great dad, but he's only human! So whether or not your father was there for you, he can't meet the need God has placed within your heart for Him alone. Let's explore the father-daughter bond—both earthly and heavenly.

Question One

God is the Father who is there. What do the following verses reveal about His relationship with you?

1. Psalm 27:10

2. Psalm 68:4–6

3. 2 Corinthians 6:18

Question Two

Many women fear abandonment because their earthly fathers were not there for them. How long will your heavenly Father walk beside you and hold you close (Isa. 9:6; John 17:3)?

Question Three

1. Read Romans 8:15–16. Your heavenly Father isn't alone in parenting you. The previous references reveal that Jesus assists. Who else works hand-in-hand with the Father?

   _____

2. Write out Romans 8:15–16, noting key words.
   a. Romans 8:15

   b. Romans 8:16

Question Four

Let's analyze Romans 8:15–16 carefully.
1. After God adopts you, He asks you to call Him *Abba* (Greek for "Daddy"). Our purpose is to explore our relationship with our Abba. What a privilege! What do little girls need from their daddies?

2. What results when little girls are not cared for in this way (8:15a)? What role has this powerful emotion played in your life?

For Reflection

Because human fathers are people, they're never perfect. How do you feel as you reminisce about your earthly father? What do you need in a heavenly Father?

3. Who bears witness that you can trust your heavenly Father (8:16)? What do you think this means?

 To learn more about your adoption and inheritance, read Romans 8:17–27. For more insight, study the entire chapter. What is the Spirit's role in our lives as God's children, especially our prayer lives?

God Is Transcendent

Although God our Father is intimate and knowable, He is also infinitely above and beyond what we can imagine or grasp. While He condescends to us, still He remains totally "Other"—mysterious, dwelling in unapproachable light. His majesty, power, and strength make Him the Father we need in the world where we find ourselves—the Father who deserves respect and who can take care of us.

Question Five

Define *transcendent,* using a dictionary.

Question Six

1. What visual picture does Job paint of God in Job 37:21–22?

2. What does he reveal about God in Job 37:23–24?

3. What does Isaiah write about God in Isaiah 55:8–9?

4. How does David express this truth in Psalm 145:3?

5. Why do you think our Father wants us to know these things about Him?

Question Seven

1. Describe how Job responds to God's transcendence (Job 42:1–6).

2. What difference does it make that you worship a heavenly Father who is transcendent?

Question Eight

Although there is a sense in which your Abba is unreachable now, what does 1 Corinthians 13:12 promise? See also Psalm 17:15. When will this happen?

Question Nine

God is transcendent—yet a Father's heart beats within Him—a heart for you! Some women grieve because they feel that their earthly fathers didn't really understand them. How well does your Abba know you? Let's find out.

1. What does your Abba know about you right now (Ps. 139:1–4)?

2. How did David feel about this fact (Ps. 139:5–6)?

3. How do you feel about the transcendent God knowing you this way?

Question Ten

1. John uses another visual picture to describe your intimate relationship with your Abba (John 10:14). What is it? What does this picture reveal about the relationship?

2. Even though your Abba knows your faults and failures, what assurance do you discover in John 10:28–30?

 What else can you learn about God's intimate knowledge of you from the following passages?
   • Acts 1:24

• 1 Corinthians 8:1–3

• Galatians 4:8–9

God Is Intimate

God the Father knows and understands you completely. And His great desire is that you would know and understand Him in response. Let's discover how you know your heavenly Father.

Question Eleven

You know your Father through creation.

1. Paraphrase the following verses. What do they say about how God has made Himself known?
   a. Psalm 19:1–4a

   b. Romans 1:18–20

2. Describe your favorite "creation" spot—or bring a picture to the group. Why is this particular place in God's creation so meaningful and beautiful to you?

Question Twelve

You know your Father through His love letter—the Bible.

1. Why did God record His love for you in a book (John 20:30–31)?

2. Can you remember receiving written words that expressed affection from your earthly father or other men in your life? If so, how did these words affect you? What did you do with them? What is your heart attitude as you read Abba's love letter to you?

 What will the Bible accomplish in you if you savor its message (2 Tim. 3:16; Heb. 4:12)?

Question Thirteen

You know your Father through Jesus Christ.

Your Abba wanted to reveal Himself to you in ways you could clearly understand—so He came and lived here in the Person of Jesus Christ.

1. What does Paul call Jesus in Colossians 1:15 and 2:2–3?

2. How does Abba reveal His love for you today? What do you learn about Him in Hebrews 1:1–3?

Question Fourteen

You know your Father through the Spirit.

1. What has your Abba given you to help you respond to His love (Ezek. 36:26–27)?

2. Read John 14:16–20, where Jesus reveals that you are not an orphan! How is Abba's perfect parenting revealed in these verses?

3. Read Romans 8:26–27. What is your primary means of communicating your affection and needs to your Abba? How does the Spirit help you?

Question Fifteen

You know your Father through changed lives.

Our relationship with our Father changes us over time. How has your life changed since your adoption? What future changes would you like to see?

1. My life before adoption.

2. Steps that led me to adoption.

3. Changes I have seen since my adoption.

4. Future changes I'd like to see.

Question Sixteen

The transcendent God is your Abba! This magnificent truth is beyond our grasp—but God declares it is *true!* He wants to know you intimately. How much do you want to know Him?

   1. What is Abba's request in Deuteronomy 4:29? What does He promise you?

   2. What else does He promise you in return (Pss. 9:10; 145:18)?

   3. What other treasure will be yours (Jer. 33:3)?

Between You and God

Will you make a covenant to seek your heavenly Father wholeheartedly during this study?

_____ I will make quality time to commune with God over my lesson.

_____ I will not allow the enemy to deter my faithful attendance.

_____ I will not allow the enemy to sow discord in my group.

_____ I will _____

Question Seventeen

Throughout our lives, we search for security and significance. As little girls we yearned for fathers who would make us feel completely safe and special. Many of us were disappointed. As a result, we sought these things in other ways.

   1. Read Jeremiah 9:23. Where do many women look for security and significance? How have you tried to feel safe and special? Have you been successful?

2. What does our Abba advise (Jer. 9:24)? Why?

3. Take some time to meditate on what you have learned about the transcendent God with a Father's heart.

> Be still, and know that I am God.
> —Psalm 46:10

Lesson 2

Abba

Worthy of Honor

My Daddy was the first man in my life—and my first hero. I couldn't wait for him to come home! I would run and jump into his arms, and he would swing me around, and I'd squeal and laugh hilariously. Beaches and ball games; the smell of grass clippings, sawdust, oil, and sweat; the feel of whiskers against my cheek, even the sight of cars—all bring back memories of him.

But these memories are scarred by other recollections: Mom pleading with him to return the money he'd "borrowed" from work; Mom catching him in lies about where he'd been and with whom; his flirting with me that turned into uncomfortable touching. More than anything, I needed someone I could look up to and respect. In time I learned he couldn't be trusted—and now, I don't seem to be able to trust anybody.

—Lorraine, thirty-seven

Like Lorraine, little girls tend to idolize their daddies, but inevitably they discover that to some degree dads aren't the invincible men who can fix anything. In some cases dads aren't even worthy of respect. A woman's future emotional, romantic, and spiritual relationships are often colored by this disappointment.

Is there anyone who can be totally trusted? Is there anyone always worthy of respect? Yes! But only *One* will never let you down—your heavenly Father!

Let's explore the character of your Abba. He alone is completely pure, good, true, incorruptible. He alone is majestic and holy. *Holy* comes from the Hebrew word "to cut" or "to separate." It refers to God's complete and total separation from evil. He alone is a Father worthy of worship.

Question One

1. What does the Bible reveal about God's character from these verses?
   a. Numbers 23:19

   b. Revelation 15:4

2. What consequences do women face when they expect any human person, including themselves, to live out holiness consistently in his or her everyday life?

3. The Scriptures sing of God's holiness. Record your insights from these marvelous passages that describe God's majesty and holiness.
   a. Exodus 3:5

   b. Exodus 15:11

   c. Leviticus 10:3

   d. Psalm 93:1, 5

   e. Psalm 96:9

   f. Psalm 99:1–3

4. What is a fitting response when we begin to grasp God's holiness?
   a. Psalm 30:4

   b. Psalm 145:5–7

 Many Bible authors enjoyed a great privilege. What was it and how would you have felt if you had been one of them (2 Peter 1:16)?

Question Two

1. Your heavenly Father alone is holy! As a result what else is true about Him (Ps. 5:4–6)?

 Isaiah paints a picture of the millennial kingdom in Isaiah 35:8–10. Describe it. What do you learn about the wicked?

2. What demand does God make of His children (Lev. 20:26; 1 Peter 1:14–15)?

3. Is it possible for us to be holy (Isa. 64:5–6; Rom. 3:9–20)? Why can't a holy God overlook impurity? List ways that people try to justify their unholiness before a holy Father.

4. Does God seem unreasonable? What is the monumental dilemma for God? What is our plight? What is God's heart toward us as we face this dilemma (Isa. 57:15–19)?

Question Three

1. What did your Abba do so you could have a parent whom you could respect and honor (Rom. 3:21–27; 5:9–11; Eph. 1:7)?

2. Although God calls us to holiness, we cannot be holy in the same way God is holy. God's holiness is an intrinsic, inherent, infinite kind of holiness. A. W. Tozer writes in *The Knowledge of the Holy*,

> God is holy with an absolute holiness that knows no degrees, and this He cannot impart to His creatures. But there is a relative and contingent holiness which He shares with angels . . . and with redeemed men on earth as their preparation for heaven. This holiness God can and does impart to His children. He shares it with them by imputation and by impartation, and because He has made it available to them through the blood of the Lamb, He requires it of them.[1]

Although we cannot be holy in the infinite way God is holy, our Abba gives us a holy position in Him while He prepares us for our eternal future together. Read Romans 6:19–22 aloud several times. How does our Father want us to cooperate with Him in this process?

3. Holiness for us means that we are members of a holy family, destined to live a distinctive lifestyle! What do we need to be holy? Jot down insights from these verses:
   a. Romans 12:1–2

   b. 1 Thessalonians 4:3–8

   c. 1 Thessalonians 5:6–8

   d. 1 Peter 1:13–15

4. Read 2 Corinthians 6:14–17. What are the warnings? What are the instructions? Does this mean Christians should withdraw from the world? What is the balance between seeking holiness and ministering to a lost world?

5. Can you be holy on your own? What is absolutely essential for holiness (Gal. 5:16, 22–26)?

6. Why is He named *Holy* Spirit and why is the Bible called the *Holy* Bible?

7. We are children of a Father worthy of respect and honor. What question does He ask us in Malachi 1:6?

8. How would you answer? As you examine your life this week, what are you doing to show Him the respect He deserves? What do you need to eliminate because it dishonors your family name?

Question Four

Isaiah was one of the greatest Old Testament prophets. God called Isaiah through an experience that is a picture of everything we have just learned. Read Isaiah 6:1–8.

1. God transported Isaiah to His throne room. Describe the scene. How would you have felt (Isa. 6:1–4)?

2. What was Isaiah's response to this holy vision (Isa. 6:5)? What does this outburst represent in the life of a Christian? Have you ever felt the same way?

3. What happened next? What did God do for Isaiah (Isa. 6:6–7)? What do you think this represents in God's dealings with His children? Has this happened to you?

4. What was God's follow-up question? How did Isaiah answer Him (Isa. 6:8)?

5. Has God asked you the same question? What is your answer and specifically what does that mean in your life right now?

Question Five

Serving with your Father to further His purposes is not duty; it is a privilege—and it is a source of great joy now and for eternity! But before you can answer God's call to serve, you must pursue holiness and attempt to live in peace with others. "Make every effort to live in peace with all men and to be holy" (Heb. 12:14).

We are called to pursue holiness with passion—and at the same time God asks us to extend mercy to ourselves and others when we fail. As little girls we expected holiness from our fathers and other significant people in our lives. But as we matured, we came to understand that no one on earth can fulfill these expectations and perfectionist ideals. Only God is a Father worthy of honor and respect. Nevertheless, our call is to seek holiness while holding out a forgiving hand.

Plato wrote, "The unexamined life is not worth living." Take time away this week to ask yourself some hard questions: Am I pursuing holiness with passion? Has someone wounded me, recently or in the past, which resulted in feelings that are hindering me from holiness? Is there someone I need to forgive so I can move on to love and serve my Abba?

A Father Who Cherishes Me

My father was the most important influence in my life. He made me believe I could achieve anything if I worked hard enough. And he made me feel terribly attractive. Whenever I'd worry about ever getting a boyfriend, he'd laugh and say, "Are you kidding? I'll have to beat off the guys with a stick. You'll see." His whole approach was to make me feel good about myself, and most of the time he succeeded. I think if fathers do nothing else, that's a great thing.

—Harriet, forty[1]

How did your father make you feel about yourself? Hopefully you are a "Harriet," but if not, there is still a Father who loves you unconditionally and always has your best interest at heart. He is your heavenly Father. He is worthy of honor and respect, even worship. He is transcendent— yet He is your Abba!

How much does He love you? Let's find out.

Question One

He is your Creator.

Did anyone ever save a picture you made, hanging it on the refrigerator as if it were a masterpiece? That's the way God feels about you. He created you! You are not the product of time and chance, a billion years of evolution, or random cells that will disintegrate into dust. You aren't an accident. You were planned!

1. How did you become who you are (Pss. 94:9; 100:3; Rev. 4:11)?

2. Do you like your body? If not, why not? Who designed it? When and where? How do you think God feels about your body? Do you and God think alike when it comes to this subject (Pss. 139:13–15; 145:17)?

3. What cultural factors influence the way you perceive your body? Contrast the way God sees your body with the way the world sees your body.

4. How much time do you spend on your "body project"? How can you look attractive and stay healthy, yet not obsess over your body? What's the balance?

5. Why did God create you (Isa. 43:7; Eph. 1:11–12)? How does God want you to carry out that purpose?

6. In Deuteronomy 32:6, God asked His children a question. What was the question and how would you answer it? Do your priorities reflect His purposes for you?

7. The Bible doesn't focus on our external appearance. In fact the only thing we know about Jesus' appearance is that "He had no beauty or majesty to attract us to him, nothing in his appearance that we should desire him" (Isa. 53:2). Why do you think God is not nearly as concerned with the external as man is?

8. What does God love about you? Does God love you more than you love yourself? If so, why do you feel this way?

Question Two

Your Father loves you unconditionally!

> My father was the type who couldn't express love—only approval or disapproval. Once I got a B on a report card, and he said, "What's this?" I said, "Why don't you say anything about all A's?" He said, "I expect that." The good news is that he trained me to be extremely capable, so I'm very successful—I can take care of myself. The downside is that I'm a driven workaholic. I can't make a mistake, and I feel as if I'm always walking on eggshells. One false move and it's all undone. I feel as if I'm only as good as my last accomplishment.
>
> —Judy, forty-three[2]

Little girls want daddies who will love them for who they are, not for their accomplishments. Yet in this fallen world, earthly parents struggle to love this way. Only God loves you perfectly.

1. Even though David failed God often, what did David know? Rather than accomplishments, what does God desire from you (Pss. 26:3; 32:10; 36:7–10)?

2. Little girls also yearn for fathers who will protect and rescue them. Because God loves you unconditionally, what did He do for you (Rom. 5:8; Eph. 2:4–6)?

3. When you are discouraged, what does your loving Father do for you (Pss. 31:7–8; 103:3–5)?

4. When you disappoint Him, how does He act (Ps. 103:10–13)?

5. Once you have experienced God's unconditional love, what is an appropriate response?

   a. Psalm 89:1–2

   b. Psalm 145:4–5

   c. Ephesians 4:1–3

   d. 1 John 4:7–12

Question Three

God's love is like a brilliant diamond, reflecting many different facets of His character. The following verses contain other words that reveal the kinds of love He bestows upon you. How is each kind of love different?

   1. Psalm 119:68

   2. Lamentations 3:21–24

   3. Nahum 1:3

4. Luke 6:35

5. 2 Corinthians 1:3

Question Four

Psalm 107 calls us to "consider the great love of the LORD" (v. 43) and gives us four kinds of people who should give thanks for their Father's loving-kindness. Read Psalm 107.

    1. How long will our Abba love us (Ps. 107:1)?

    2. How can we please our Father (Ps. 107:1–2a)?

    3. Where do our siblings come from? What are the implications (Ps. 107:3)?

Question Five

The first group (Ps. 107:4–9).

    1. Identify and name the first group of people: _____

    2. What happened to them? How did they feel? What did they do? How did their Father rescue them?

3. Can you, in any sense, relate to this group? If so, please share the circumstances and how God helped or is currently helping you.

Question Six

The second group (Ps. 107:10–16).

1. Name the second group: _____

2. How are they different from the first group?

3. What did their Father require before He rescued them? What did He do for them?

4. Are you also imprisoned? If so, how? Has God "cut through bars of iron for you"?

Question Seven

The third group (Ps. 107:17–22).

1. Name this group: _____

2. Why are they suffering? In what ways do they express their anguish? What did God do to heal them?

3. Are you like these people in any way? Have you ever been? If so, how?

Question Eight

The fourth group (Ps. 107:23–32).

   1. Name these kinds of people: _____

   2. What kind of people set sail on the high seas? Maybe you've never served on a ship's crew, but in what sense are you like or unlike this group?

   3. Describe their experience at first.

   4. What happened later? What did they do and how did God answer?

Question Nine

A benevolent Father (Ps. 107:33–43).

   1. Now the poet sketches pictures of God's blessings on His children. Describe the good gifts the Father bestows upon His own.

2. What happens in verses 39–40? Why do we sometimes experience "oppression, calamity and sorrow" in our lives?

3. Nevertheless, how does Abba ultimately bless His children (107:41–42)?

4. The author ends with a command in verse 43. What is it and why do you think your Father makes this request?

5. Have you accepted "the great love of the Lord" for yourself? If so, thank Him however your heart leads. If not, confess your doubts and ask your heavenly Father to help you. Share how you feel with the group.

 Over and over in the Bible, God illustrates His love for His own. Do a character study, focusing on the ways God showed His loving-kindness to the following people:
- Lot (Gen. 19)

- Jacob (Gen. 27–35)

- Esther

- Ruth

- Rahab (Josh. 2)

- The Ninevites (Jonah)

- Paul

- Peter

- Epaphroditus (Phil. 2:25–30)

Question Ten

For personal reflection.

You are God's creation—cherished and adored. This holy "Other"—perfection in His Person, kindness in His acts—is your Abba. He died for you in the Person of Christ so that you could live with Him forever and experience joy now.

Will you treasure His love and live in it? Will you accept yourself as God created you and, out of gratitude, extend His grace to others? Will you live to please Him, knowing that when you do, you will also bless yourself? Your answers make all the difference!

A Father I Can Count On!

Last week you discovered a heavenly Father who cherishes you and cares deeply about the needs in your life. But is He a Father who can act on your behalf? Does He really understand the complexities of your problems and know the wisest course of action? Will He step out and do something when it's appropriate? Can you trust Him? Some women have greater struggles than others trusting God.

A Tale of Two Women

Family always came first for my father. When I was little, he would drive me to school every morning on his way to work. The day I started kindergarten, I was terrified—I took his hat so he couldn't leave. He peered through a glass door, waving and smiling every time I looked up at him. Finally I started playing with the other kids and let go of the hat. He did that for five days in a row, until I wasn't afraid anymore and he could just drop me off. He never got annoyed, not once. That's my daddy.

—Milly, forty-three[1]

My parents divorced when I was five, and ever since the world has never been a safe place. Divorce teaches you that one morning everything can be fine and by nighttime the earth can fall apart. It teaches you never to count on anyone but yourself. It teaches you not to invest too much in anyone, because they could always leave.

—Paula, thirty-nine[2]

Will Milly or Paula have the greater struggle trusting God? Are you more like Milly or Paula? Richard Strauss writes, "Many of us have had disillusioning experiences with people who have promised more than they have been able to deliver, and we have a tendency to transfer our skepticism to God. Does He really have the power to bring good out of adversity? Our doubts serve no purpose but to raise our anxiety level and cause us grief. God is able to do whatever needs to be done in your life."[3] Are you fully convinced?

Last week we compared God's love to a brilliant diamond, examining the different aspects of His loving-kindness. Let's look again at the many-faceted brilliance of God—but this time let's focus on His ability.

Question One

Omnipresent—He is everywhere!

1. How big is your God? What are the questions God asks in Jeremiah 23:23–24? How would you answer Him?

2. In contrast, what does the Bible teach about man (James 4:14)?

3. Isaiah understood the vastness of God. What's the visual image in Isaiah 66:1? What do you learn about the immensity of God?

4. In 2 Chronicles 16:9 and Proverbs 15:3, the Bible speaks metaphorically of "the eyes of the LORD." Where do they look? Why?

5. Do you tend to limit God's place to the church or other special "holy" sites? What does 1 Kings 8: 27 reveal?

6. Read Psalm 139:7–12. According to this passage, specifically what is God and where is He? Do you think the psalmist is fearful or glad that his Father is there?

7. Was your earthly father absent or passive? How about others you counted on? If so, how did you feel as a child? How have you been affected as a woman? Why is it significant that no matter where you go or how you might try to evade your Abba, He is always there?

Question Two

Omniscience—He knows all about it!

God may be everywhere and see everything, but does He really understand the complexities of *my* life?

1. What does God know about the world from beginning to end (Heb. 4:13; Rev. 1:8)?

2. What does God know about us?
   a. 1 Chronicles 28:9

   b. Job 23:10

   c. Psalm 44:20–21

   d. Psalm 139:1–6

   e. Luke 12:7

3. Does God tell us everything that He knows? What are we to do with what He reveals (Deut. 29:29)?

Question Three

Omnipotence—He is able!

Although God is everywhere and understands everything, even the intricate details, does He have the power to act? Can He do anything to make a difference?

> One night when I was eight, my dad took us to the movies. He's a strong, silent type—rugged and very tall. Some kids behind us were making a lot of noise. My mom asked them to be quiet, and they said, "Shut your mouth, lady!" My father slowly rose to his feet, turned around and said, "Excuse me?" The kids ran like mad out of the theater. I remember feeling so happy my dad was there—so protected and so safe.
>
> —Doris, thirty-five[4]

> God's power is like Himself, self-existent, self-sustained. The mightiest of men cannot add so much as a shadow of increased power to the Omnipotent One. He sits on no buttressed throne and leans on no assisting arm. His court is not maintained by His courtiers, nor does it borrow its splendor from His creatures. He is Himself the great central source and originator of all power.
>
> —C. H. Spurgeon[5]

1. Read Psalm 18:7–15. Describe the scene. What was God's mood? How did He express it?

2. Now describe the scene in verses 16 through 19. How was the author feeling?

3. Has God ever rescued you? Can you relate to the psalmist's account? If so, share the experience with your group.

4. Parents, friends, family, and counselors often want to help in our struggles. What can they do for us? What are their limitations? When should we go to people? When should we go to God? Share any related experiences.

5. According to the wise man Agur, what does God have the power to do (Prov. 30:1–4)? How does Agur feel as he contemplates these truths? What is your response?

6. How does David describe God's power in Psalm 147:3–6. What does God do with His power?

7. What does Jehoshaphat proclaim about God's power (2 Chron. 20:6)? How does this verse affect your view of politics?

 What does Abraham testify about God's ability (Rom. 4:16–21)?

 What do Paul and Peter teach about God's power?
- Ephesians 1:18–20

- 1 Peter 1:3–5

 Job argued with God that he did not deserve the hardships he was enduring. God answered him in Job 38 through 42, beginning with the words, "Who is this that darkens my counsel with words without knowledge? Brace yourself like a man; I will question you and you shall answer me." For a breathtaking look at God's infinite power, read the chapters and record your thoughts.

Question Four

Immutable—God does not change.

I really had four relationships with my father: The first was when I was a little girl and he just adored me. Then there were my teens, when he was always working, and when he was around, all we did was fight. Then after I got married, we were sort of polite strangers. But the last relationship was when he was sick and old—that was quite different. He was so vulnerable that you couldn't do anything but love him. I really got his tenderness and who he was; his courage and his character came through. We came full circle. I felt such completion.

—Sylvia, fifty-one[6]

1. People are a contradiction. One day you can count on them; the next day you can't find them. Describe a time when someone disappointed you. (No names, please!) How did you feel?

2. Why can you count on Abba (Pss. 89:34; 102:25–28; James 1:17)?

Question Five

In this lesson we have seen that our heavenly Father is "able to do immeasurably more than all we ask or imagine, according to His power" (Eph. 3:20). And we learned in our last lesson that He treasures us and always has our best interest at heart. He cares *and* He is able!

Then why do bad things happen in our lives? Why doesn't He always answer our prayers the way we want Him to? What is God doing in the world? We will tackle these complex questions in the lessons that follow.

1. For now, list the problems in your life that seem impossible:

2. How do you want them solved? Are you willing to allow God to solve them in His own way?

3. Begin praying that God will help you trust Him with these heartaches, and that you will come to understand His character in a way that enables you to let Him work them out in His time and in His way.

Well may the saint trust such a God! He is worthy of implicit confidence. Nothing is too hard for Him. If God were stinted in might and had a limit to His strength we might well despair. But seeing that He is clothed with omnipotence, no prayer is too hard for Him to answer, no need too great for Him to supply, no passion too strong for Him to subdue, no temptation too powerful for Him to deliver from, no misery too deep for Him to relieve. Jesus said, "With God all things are possible" (Matt. 19:26).

—Arthur Pink[7]

Lesson 5

"Father Knows Best"

God's Sovereignty

Whenever I felt like falling apart, I would think of my dad. His strength was constant. When I was a kid, I was in an automobile accident, and the doctors said I'd be in a wheelchair for life. My father said, "She will walk again." He was so determined, so inspiring, that I did. At times I resented him, because we were both stubborn. But I adored him and he adored me. All the qualities that have gotten me through the hard times I got from him. I always have a voice in my head that says, "You can do it. Press on."

—Wendy, forty-five[1]

This kind of father drags his children, sometimes kicking and screaming, into giving their personal best. For he has his eye not simply on the moment but on the future—he very much wants to prepare them for survival and happiness in the adult world, to see life as a series of challenging opportunities.

To that end he is willing to be the family heavy if necessary; he is seldom plagued by second thoughts and cannot be bamboozled. He doesn't expect always to be liked, but since he tempers his demands with affection, it's hard to hate him. For he is also able to express pride in his children's accomplishments, to share their joy, to allow them to be who they are—regardless of gender.

The consensus among experts is that children of authoritarian fathers (or mothers) have the fewest behavioral problems and self-doubts. They know they can depend on him; they know where they stand. They can count on his love, support and interest as well as his discipline, the blend of which gives them enormous security. This rock-sure, loving authority has long-lasting, beneficial effects on his daughters.

—Victoria Secunda[2]

Research in this secular book insists loving authoritarians make the best fathers. This description is the closest men can come to God—the perfect, loving Authority. The Bible describes Him as sovereign, with a right to rule and with a perfect plan for the world and each of us.

Can we completely understand our Sovereign God? We live every moment of our lives as finite beings, bound by time and space, limited in our knowledge and abilities. As such, attempting to conceive of One who is sovereign and infinite is like trying to hold the ocean in a teacup. Yet our Father invites us to drink as much as we can.

Question One

1. With the help of a dictionary, define *sovereign*.

2. Living in a democracy, we find it difficult to relate to a "sovereign" ruler. Our culture teaches us in a variety of ways to undermine authority. List some of those ways. Why do you think authority is so out of fashion?

3. How do you feel about giving anyone absolute rule over you and your life? What is your attitude toward authority?

Question Two

His plans and purposes.

> God is perfection and, in an entirely unique manner, knows Himself and all things possible and actual in one eternal and most simple act.
>
> —Louis Berkhof [3]

God has eternal knowledge of His plan—past, present, and future. In creating the universe, He could have chosen among myriads of plans with their infinite varieties, with different types of life and different galaxies, but He chose this plan—and it's a perfect plan.

1. God's plan for the ages is steadily moving forward. What can you learn about God and His plan from the following verses?
   a. Deuteronomy 10:14

   b. Psalm 33:6–11

    c. Psalm 103:19

    d. Isaiah 14:24, 26–27

    e. Isaiah 46:9–10

2. Moses wanted to understand God. Read Exodus 33:18–20. What did Moses ask God? What did God show and tell Moses about Himself? Does God need to explain Himself or His actions to anyone? Why was Moses unable to see all of God?

3. King Nebuchadnezzar came to realize that God alone was sovereign. What did he say in Daniel 4:35? Describe his heart attitude.

4. How certain are God's plans (Isa. 55:10–11)?

5. Read Psalm 139:16 and Jeremiah 29:11. Describe God's personal plan for you. How do you feel as you read these verses?

Question Three

The Potter and the clay.

Often God's plans and purposes are difficult to comprehend from our perspective. Sometimes we fuss and fight with God when we don't like what's happening. God has an answer for us. Have you ever seen a potter create a clay pot on a potter's wheel? This illustration can help us when we want to "kick against the goads."

1. Who is the Potter and who is the clay? What is God doing to us on the wheel (Isa. 64:8)?

2. What is a common reaction when we don't like the shape we are in (Isa. 29:16)?

3. What is the warning in Isaiah 45:9–12? Does this mean we should never express our feelings to God? What is the heart attitude God desires?

4. Does God have the right to shape His own pots? To rule His own world? What does He proclaim in Isaiah 45:6–8?

5. Job's experience on the Potter's wheel was excruciating, and he vocalized his misery to the Potter repeatedly. But after Job understood the Potter's sovereignty, what was his response (Job 42:1–6)? What helped Job come to this conclusion?

6. How do you think the pot feels on the wheel? Do you like the way the Potter is working on you? Do you think He can make something beautiful? Please share your perspective from the wheel right now.

7. If we are miserable on the wheel, what does God ask us to do anyway (1 Peter 4:19)?

Question Four

 God reveals His plan for Israel in Romans 9–11, drawing back the curtain on His sovereignty in the process. Note Paul's use of the illustration of the potter and his arguments from history. What is God's plan for the Jews, and what do you learn about His supremacy in these chapters?

Question Five

Election.

One of the most perplexing concepts in God's plan is "election." Although the doctrine of election is beyond human comprehension, it is clearly in the Bible, as we will see.

1. Why did Abba adopt you as His daughter? When? What is your future as a result?

   a. John 15:16

   b. Ephesians 1:4–6

c. 2 Timothy 1:8–9

d. 1 Peter 1:1–2

2. By divine election, God has chosen certain individuals for salvation and predestined them to be His children eternally, ultimately conformed to the character of His Son Jesus Christ. The choice originated with God and is part of His sovereign plan. On what basis did God make His choices (1 Cor. 1:18–31)? Why (v. 31)?

3. Who else is part of God's plan of election (1 Tim. 5:21)?

 List all the references to election in Matthew 24, where Jesus teaches His followers about the end times. What part will the elect play in the tribulation?

Question Six

Sovereignty, free will, and human responsibility.

1. Why is Paul giving thanks in 2 Thessalonians 2:13? What part did God play? What part did the Thessalonians play in their salvation? In this verse, we observe a tension between God's sovereignty and human responsibility that is beyond our ability to completely understand. What is this tension?

2. Write out Acts 2:22–23 in which Peter is preaching to thousands of Jews. From verse 23, what two factors brought about Jesus' crucifixion? Again, what is the tension?

   a. Acts 2:22

   b. Acts 2:23

3. As part of God's sovereign plan, what did He choose to give His creatures (Gen. 2:16; 2 Cor. 3:17)?

4. What would our relationship to our Father look like if this had not been His intention? Why do you think He designed His plan this way?

Behold a Mystery . . .

Grasping the concepts of election, free will, and human responsibility is difficult. It is obvious from experience as well as from Scripture that people have choices. How can one avoid thinking in terms of a fatalistic system where everything is predetermined and no moral choices are left? Is human responsibility just a mockery or is it real? Are our choices real even if God already knows what we will choose?

To God, the plan is already accomplished. He is not bound by time as we are. When you watch a football game for which you already know the outcome, your knowledge doesn't affect the actual choices the players make in the game. Just because God sees and knows what choices we will make, doesn't mean He makes them for us.

For example, the whole plan of God hinged on the crucifixion of Christ. However, Pilate freely made a choice to crucify Jesus, and Pilate was held responsible for his decision. Judas Iscariot freely determined to betray Christ and was held responsible for that decision. Yet God knew what Pilate and Judas would choose before the foundation of the world. Those choices were part of God's program.

While theologians have never been able to resolve completely the problem of divine election as related to human choice and man's responsibility, the answer seems to be that in choosing a plan,

God chose the plan as a whole. He is not limited by time. As a result, He knew in advance who would be saved and who would not. By faith, we must assume that God chose the best possible plan, and that if a better plan could have been put into operation, God would have chosen it.

Much of the plan included what God would do Himself, such as creation and the establishment of natural law. It included what God sovereignly chose to do Himself on earth. He came to earth in the form of Jesus as teacher and redeemer. He gave us the Scriptures. And He indwells His own by His Spirit. Through these and other means, God influences men in their choices, even though they are free to choose and are responsible for the choices they make.

In other words, the plan included giving man some freedom of choice for which he would then be held responsible. The fact that God knew the plan and what each man would do does not mean that God forced man to do something against his will. Accordingly, while these concepts are beyond our understanding, the best solution is to accept what the Bible teaches, whether or not we understand it completely. In His mystery and majesty, we can worship a sovereign King who has chosen to call us His own, knowing His ways are higher than our ways and always for our good.

> Oh, the depth of the riches of the wisdom
> and knowledge of God!
> How unsearchable his judgments,
> and his paths beyond tracing out!
> Who has known the mind of the Lord?
> Or who has been his counselor?
> Who has ever given to God,
> that God should repay him?
> For from him and through him and
> to him are all things.
> To him be the glory forever! Amen.
> —Romans 11:33–36

My "Jealous" Father

This world can be a frightening, evil place. Little girls need involved fathers who guide and protect, who provide sensible boundaries and discipline, who shelter them from unhealthy influences and boisterous beaus with suspicious intentions. When fathers are absent, passive, harsh, or unreasonable, we don't receive this firm, yet loving guidance—and often we falter as women. Listen to Carole and Corrie express the effects on their lives:

> One of my earliest memories of my father was when I was four. I woke up in the middle of the night and saw these scary shapes on my window shade and screamed, "Daddy, Daddy!" He rushed in, sat on the edge of the bed, and explained that it was just the streetlight playing tricks and that everything was all right. He stayed with me until I fell back to sleep. I remember thinking, "When I grow up, will I ever find a man as sweet and good and kind as my daddy?" So far, I haven't.
>
> —Carole, thirty[1]

> No one ever told me not to express my feelings as a kid. From day one I just knew not to. I'm like my dad that way. I never had an identity, not really, and because I don't, what I do is meaningless. I never realize the consequences of my actions, whether it's not paying my bills, or binge eating, or getting involved with rotten men. I'm never aware of the reality until it's literally hitting me over the head, like when the IRS closed my bank account. It's like I don't exist. I feel as if I could disappear from the earth, and no one would ever notice.
>
> —Corrie, thirty-two[2]

Even though you may have had a father more like Corrie's, now you have a heavenly Father who takes an active role in your life—in your affections, your decisions, your loyalties, your past, and your future. Like a father who greets the would-be suitor at the door with "Five Simple Rules for Dating My Daughter," your heavenly Father has a passionate, voracious zeal for your best interests. This week we dig deep into the character of our protective, jealous Abba.

Question One

A protective Father.

1. List your Father's promises, noting specific areas of care and the authors' imagery.
   a. Psalm 3:3

b. Psalm 4:8

c. Psalm 32:7

d. Psalm 84:11

e. Psalm 116:6–7

f. Psalm 116:15

g. Psalm 145:14–15

h. Matthew 6:26

i. 2 Thessalonians 3:3

2. Your Abba doesn't protect everyone. What does He expect from His children (Pss. 33:18, 20; 91:14–15; Prov. 2:7; 30:5)?

 Read Psalms 5; 121; and 2 Samuel 22 to see three exquisite expressions of God's guardianship. (The last passage is David's song of praise when the Lord delivers him from Saul.) Record your impressions.

Question Two

A Jealous Father.

In Othello, Shakespeare describes jealousy as "a green-eyed monster." Human jealousy smacks of resentment, spite, or envy because "I want what you've got." Many of us picture the lunatic ravings of an insecure boyfriend or husband if his "woman" engages in innocent conversation with another man. In contrast, God's jealousy is a righteous jealousy. J. I. Packer writes that God's jealousy is "His holiness reacting to evil in a way that is morally right and glorious—a praiseworthy zeal to preserve something precious."[3]

God birthed the nation Israel as His special people, loving them with the tenderness of a devoted Father or Husband. He expected them to be a witness to the surrounding nations and to show those nations the beauty of intimate communion with the God of the universe. His relationship with the Jews (also called Israel, Judah, Jerusalem, and Jacob) in the Old Testament is an object lesson for us.

1. What does God call Himself in Deuteronomy 4:24; Nahum 1:2; and Zechariah 1:14?

2. What instructions did God give His children? What did He name Himself (Exod. 34:12–14)?

3. What did His children do to arouse His jealousy (1 Kings 14:22–24; Ps. 78:58)?

4. Today we don't worship wooden idols on hills or mountains; we do, nevertheless, worship idols. What modern-day "idols"—dangers and unhealthy influences—concern parents today? How do they attempt to guide and protect their children?

5. What personal "idols" concern your Abba right now? What steals your devotion to Him? What might put you in danger?

6. Your Father wants you home and eating dinner with Him. What is the imagery and contrast in 1 Corinthians 10:18–22? Is there any area of your life where you are even subtly "eating dinner with demons"?

7. Why is your Abba so upset about the "idols" in your life (Ps. 135:4; Isa. 42:8)?

Question Three

The story of the adopted and adulterous wife.

Read Ezekiel 16. This is a parable depicting Israel first as God's adopted daughter and, later, as His unfaithful wife.

1. Who were her parents? How did they treat her (Ezek. 16:1–5)?

2. Who took her in? What would have happened if He had passed her by? What kind of care did she receive in His family (Ezek. 16:6–7)?

3. As she grew into womanhood, how did He protect and adorn her (Ezek. 16:8–13a)?

4. As a result, what kind of life was provided for her (Ezek. 16:13b–14)?

5. Despite all of the advantages she had been given, what did she do with her privilege and blessing (Ezek. 16:15–21)? In what sense does she represent the detestable practices of Israel?

 The prophet Jeremiah also wrote about an ungrateful, unfaithful woman. Read Jeremiah 2:20–28. What poetic language does he use to describe her rebellion?

6. What had she forgotten (Ezek. 16:22)? How do you think God feels today when His children act like this woman?

7. How was she even worse than a prostitute (Ezek. 16:30–34)? What was God saying about His own?

8. What did her harlotry cost her (Ezek. 16:35–42)? How do you think God was feeling as He disciplined her? Was this too harsh or actually a loving thing to do? Did she deserve what happened to her?

9. After He disciplined her, what did He do (Ezek. 16:59–60, 62–63)? See also Isaiah 25:6–8 and 40:1–2.

10. What has God done so that we can experience our Father's compassion and ultimate blessing (Rom. 3:21–26; 5:8–9)?

11. What is the purpose of the Father's discipline (Heb. 12:5–11)?

12. Ezekiel 16 first pictures the relationship between God and Israel in the Old Testament. But we can make valid applications concerning our relationship with God today. What has this parable taught you about the God who calls Himself "Jealous"?

The story of the "O" sisters.

Read Ezekiel 23. What happened to the "O" Sisters? Contrast and compare this story with the parable in Ezekiel 16. What additional insight do you glean regarding the nature of our jealous Father?

The song of Moses.

Study Deuteronomy 32:1–43. What sections enrich your understanding of God as a jealous and protective Father? What verses foreshadow Gentile inclusion and the consummation of biblical history?

The story of a man who married a harlot to teach us about God's jealousy.

Read the book of Hosea. What does Hosea's relationship with Gomer teach us about God's relationship with Israel and with us?

Question Four

1. In the passages we've studied, your heavenly Father has revealed Himself as caring and protective, yet jealous, in a righteous sort of way. Has anyone ever loved you this way? Are you glad He loves you this much—or does it make you afraid? If you are a woman who has never been loved this intensely, how does this love make you feel?

2. As you contemplate what you've learned in this lesson, what is your Abba saying to you? Can you think of any actions or attitudes on your part that might be arousing His jealousy? If so, confess them to God. Be specific. Now ask for the strength to turn from them. Remember, He is quick to forgive and delights in your repentance. More than anything, He is a Father who wants to bless you!

A Father Who Is Fair

We yearned for fairness from our earthly fathers. When we fought with our siblings we wanted someone who could sort out the truth, arbitrate fairly, and not play favorites. We needed to know that the ground rules wouldn't change on a whim.

> When I was around nine, my father said he would pay me five dollars if I could do a handstand for a full minute. I practiced and I practiced and I practiced, because I so wanted to please him and make him proud of me. Finally I was able to do a real handstand, and I showed him. He said, "Okay, here's the five dollars. But from now on, you have to be able to do it *anytime* I ask. If you can't, you have to give me the money back." And then he laughed. It just killed me.
>
> —Linda, forty-one[1]

All of us, either as children, parents, or on a school playground, have heard the anguished plea, "But it's not fair!" You probably still feel that way sometimes. The demand for fairness is inborn; we don't have to teach children the concept. It's part of being made in the image of God. Whether or not your earthly father was fair, your Abba is just and righteous as part of His moral perfection. He, too, yearns for life to be fair—and it isn't—but it will be! He has the power to make justice roll down like a mighty river (Amos 5:24). When that day arrives, all wrongs will be righted and we'll feel totally secure for the first time. He's a Father that can make it right!

But when? Let's find out.

Question One

Where is justice?

1. Why was Habakkuk complaining to God (Hab. 1:2–4)?

2. How did the Jews express the same frustration (Isa. 59:9–11)?

3. What are some of the reasons there is so little justice on the earth (Isa. 59:12–15a)?

4. What is your Abba's response to injustice, first for His own children and then to those who reject Him (Isa. 59:15b–21; 1 Thess. 5:9)?

Study the widow's plea for justice in Luke 18:1–8. What was Jesus teaching His followers through this parable?

In Psalm 73, Asaph laments that the wicked prosper. What is his ultimate conclusion?

5. Can you remember a time when you cried out for justice? If so, please share your experience with the group.

6. In America we enjoy a society and judicial system that is, in many ways, the envy of other nations. Nevertheless, is there injustice in this system? Discuss specific examples.

7. Can you name other countries or peoples who cry out against injustice every day? What is happening to them? Who are their current oppressors? Past oppressors?

Question Two

Cry for justice.

    1. What do these verses reveal about the world's plea for justice, the Judge, and the justice He promises?

        a. Psalm 7:6–9

        b. Psalm 11

        c. Psalm 36:6

        d. Psalm 37:6

        e. Psalm 45:6

        f. Isaiah 11:1–5

    2. To whom has the Father delegated justice? Why has God done this (John 5:22–30; Rom. 2:16)?

Question Three

Let justice roll down!

Some recoil from the idea of God as Judge, assuming that His love exempts Him from administering justice. But would a God who didn't care about righteousness and justice be admirable? What kind of a Father would He be?

"It is unthinkable that God would do wrong, that the Almighty would pervert justice," said Job in 34:12. "Will not the Judge of all the earth do right?" asked Abraham in Genesis 18:25. He simply must judge evil! It is part of His ethical character.

We must not forget, however, that God takes "no pleasure in the death of the wicked, but rather that they would turn from their ways and live" (Ezek. 33:11).

1. What will His justice look like? Read Psalm 97.

    a. Describe the scene (Ps. 97:1–6).

    b. How will those who reject God feel (Ps. 97:7)?

    c. How will those who love God feel (Ps. 97:8–12)?

2. The consummation of God's justice on the earth occurs at the end of the tribulation, just before Jesus returns with His children to set up His kingdom. The earth must be holy! Read Revelation 18. "Babylon" symbolizes all God's enemies and their world systems.

    a. Why is the angel rejoicing in Revelation 18:2 and 21?

    b. Describe God's enemies and their world systems (Rev. 18:2–3, 7).

c. How long will it take for God to completely annihilate Babylon (Rev. 18:17)?

d. How will God's enemies react (Rev. 18:9, 11–19)?

e. Why will Babylon be judged?

3. Why will there be great rejoicing in heaven? Describe the scene (Rev. 19:1–3). How will you feel as you witness these events?

Question Four

In the meantime . . .

1. For now injustice reigns. Why doesn't the Judge administer justice now (Nah. 1:3; 2 Peter 3:15)?

2. How shall we then live?
   a. Isaiah 30:18

   b. Zechariah 7:9–10

c. 2 Corinthians 5:11

d. Hebrews 12:28–29

3. While meditating on his Father's justice, David wrote Psalm 101, pledging a godly lifestyle while waiting for God to set things right. Read the Psalm out loud. List David's promises to God in your own words.

4. In light of the truths you are learning, are you willing to make this kind of pledge to your Abba? If so, which two are your highest priorities? What will you do this week to honor your pledge?

Injustice leaves many people suffering, and Paul was one of them. Read Romans 8:18–25.
- What was Paul's attitude toward this injustice (Rom. 8:18)?

- For what is creation yearning in Romans 8:19 and 21? What do you think Paul means?

- Who first subjected creation to injustice? How did it happen (Gen. 3:17–19; Rom. 8:20)?

- What is the state of the world right now? What picture does Paul paint to illustrate this truth (Rom. 8:22)?

- What was Paul waiting for? What are we waiting for? In what sense has this already happened? In what sense is it still unfulfilled (Rom. 8:23)?

- What are we to do while we yearn and hope for justice (Rom. 8:25)? Meditate on the truth that your Abba is ultimately fair. How do you feel as a result?

Question Five

If you aren't sure how to escape the coming wrath . . .

What is required of all who want to escape His justice? On our own, we can't escape, but God provided a way. What is it (John 5:24; Rom. 5:8; Heb. 11:6)? If this is your heart's desire, God welcomes you into His family. Now you have the Father you've always wanted.

Question Six

Let's praise Him!

Our Abba is fair, just, and righteous! Read Psalm 98 aloud to Him. Put it to music if you can. Your future is secure and bright. Your days here are fleeting and will soon blend into eternal ecstasy. Your Abba has you tight in His holy arms forever. Praise Him, all the earth! For He alone is worthy.

Question Seven

If you can't get enough . . .

In our last lesson, I asked you to read the Song of Moses in Deuteronomy 32. Read it again, but this time focus on verses 39–43 and the way they relate to the entire song and especially to God's justice.

Question Eight

If you still can't get enough . . .

Trace God's majestic plan through the book of Joel. There is no end to the depth of God's Word. Savor, enjoy, and live in light of what you've learned!

Lesson 8

"Here Is Your God"

Isaiah 40:9

Our study has painted a biblical portrait of the one, true God. He is our Abba, the personal name that we are privileged to use and that illustrates the intimate nature of our sacred relationship. As our Creator, He cherishes us and always has our best interest at heart. When we began this study, many of us were aware that God loves us; but, as we went along, some were surprised by other attributes of our heavenly Father. Not only is He an adoring Father, but He is also worthy of our deepest respect and honor because He is holy and glorious. And, unlike human fathers, He is able to take care of us because He is omnipresent, omniscient, omnipotent, and unchanging. Our bond is eternal, and we are safe in His everlasting arms.

As our Sovereign, He has the right to rule our lives, but submitting to Him is different than submitting to an earthly father. God alone is the perfect blend of tough and tender. His infinite care brings out a righteous jealousy that guards our paths and protects us from danger. And He's fair—not only now but also in the future, as He brings history to a culminating climax that ends in the creation of a perfect place for us to dwell together. This is our God!

Complete this review exercise and then we'll apply what we've learned.

Question One

Isaiah 40 is a divine masterpiece, containing multiple descriptions of our heavenly Father. Study the passage. Below are a list of the attributes we covered in our study. Beside each, write the verse or verses that relate. One verse may contain several attributes. See how many you can find.

1. glorious, holy: _____

2. creator: _____

3. loving-kindness: _____

4. omnipresent (everywhere): _____

5. omniscient (knowing all): _____

6. omnipotent (all-powerful): _____

7. immutable (eternal, unchanging): _____

70

8. sovereign: _____

9. protective: _____

10. jealous: _____

11. just: _____

Question Two

Rediscover your Father.

> I think it's possible to understand your father. But first you have to work through your feelings to reach some kind of resolution. That's what I'm trying to do—because, where men are concerned, I feel like a prisoner of my relationship with him. You know what's really crazy? I love my father—but I hate him, too. It's very confusing, and very sad. I'm just never relaxed with men, and I'm tired of it. I don't want to live the rest of my life this way.
>
> —Peg, thirty-two[1]

I hope that as you completed the lessons, you thought about your relationship with both your earthly father and heavenly Father—because one does effect the other, whether we realize it or not. As you complete this study ask yourself, "Are there unresolved issues between me and my earthly father that are keeping me from a healthy, intimate relationship with my Abba?" If so, deal with these roadblocks! If you need to forgive your earthly father, do it. If you're still holding on to unrealistic expectations, let them go. If you seem unable to overcome these problems, ask for help. Your relationship with others, and especially men, is at stake—and even more important, your relationship with your heavenly Father is eternally affected.

Here are some questions that might "prime the pump":

1. How often do you think about your earthly father?

2. Describe your relationship. Polite? Distant? Damaged? Warm?

3. What kind of relationship would you like to have with him?

4. What is the possibility of developing this relationship?

5. Is there anything you've done to sabotage the relationship? Anything you can do to improve it?

6. Do you have any regrets? What can you do about them now?

7. Are you still in bondage to any of the disappointments you experienced as a little girl? If so, how can you be free?

8. If your dad is still living, what would you like to talk about with your dad before he dies?

9. How has your relationship with your earthly father affected your relationship with men?

10. How has your relationship with your dad affected your relationship with your heavenly Father, either positively or negatively?

11. Have you accepted the reality that your earthly father isn't perfect? In what ways is your father least like your heavenly Father? Have you forgiven him?

12. How has your view of God changed as a result of this study? What have you learned to help you distinguish between your earthly father and heavenly Father? How can you build on what you've learned? Healthy relationships require investments of time, energy, and focus. What can you do now to ensure healthy relationships in your life—with your earthly father and your heavenly Father?

Training Guide for Small-Group Leaders

Studying God's Word together is an exciting adventure, requiring a leader. Thank you for your willingness to lead the group. Your role as leader is to guide a discussion characterized by

- a nonthreatening climate conducive to an honest exchange of ideas;

- a flow of stimulating and meaningful interaction;

- the presentation of God-honoring, biblically based insight.

What can you do to help the group succeed?

1. Put the Women at Ease

Express care for the women from the moment the first woman walks in the door until the last woman leaves. Greet them as they arrive. Initiate conversation before the discussion begins. Draw out women by asking nonthreatening questions such as "How long have you lived here?" or "Tell me a little about yourself." Especially focus on the woman who seems shy or lonely. Provide name tags to help women learn each other's names. Set an atmosphere of unconditional love and inclusion where women can relax, learn, and share.

- *Be other-centered!* This is not the time to visit with your best friend. You are your group's shepherdess! Many women are in dreary circumstances and have varied spiritual needs. Make walking into your group a highlight of their week!

- *Develop good listening skills.* By intentional, focused listening, you convey that the participation of each group member is valued.

You may be the only reflection of Christ some women ever see!

2. Begin and End on Time

Get started on time even if only two or three women are there. Late arrivals will soon learn they must be prompt. There will always be stragglers. Begin without them. Quickly and graciously greet them when they arrive. And honor women's busy lives by ending when you said you would, but allow women who want more fellowship to remain behind and enjoy visiting.

3. Begin with Enthusiasm

Ask someone who is enthusiastic to answer the first question. Get off to an exciting start! Keep your eyes off your study guide as much as possible. Look at the women as they are speaking. Train yourself not to read lesson notes or the introductory paragraph word for word but instead rephrase it and speak it out in your own words.

4. Assume Authority (but Remain Gracious)

- Be firm but not bossy.

- Be gentle but stay in control.

Someone has to be in charge, and you are it! The women expect you to lead. Project your voice if you are soft-spoken. Sit up and direct the group. You are there to keep the group on target and make sure time is not wasted. This is a serious role but don't forget to maintain your sense of humor and have fun.

5. Encourage Discussion: DO NOT LECTURE!

The discussion group leader is *not* a lecturer. After the discussion, you may want to wrap up the study with a formal lecture, but during the discussion the leader does not teach. She does not spotlight herself as the one with the answers but instead focuses on the women in the group. Her role is

- to direct the flow of the discussion;

- to encourage interaction;

- to set the climate or tone;

- to guard against poor use of time;

- to lead the group in an understanding of the material.

Establish an atmosphere of unconditional acceptance where each member is free to share what she is thinking and feeling. We may not always agree with a woman's view, but we can respect her by listening thoughtfully to her ideas.

As a leader you do not correct or "straighten out" women in the group. Avoid saying "No," or "But . . ." Rather, some possible responses when you hear an unusual answer are,

- "I've never thought of it in that way."

- "That's an interesting perspective."

- "I see what you're saying."

We want an atmosphere in which each woman shares what the Holy Spirit is teaching her through God's Word. Women need to feel they can ask their questions and not be made to feel foolish.

It is also imperative, though, that a biblical perspective be presented. When the group needs to hear a biblical answer, draw out women with solid biblical insight to present their views. In this way, women hear the biblical perspective, but no one in the group is singled out as the one with the wrong answer. As women continue studying the Bible, they soon discover God's perspectives for themselves.

6. Consider Calling on the Women by Name

This is better than asking for a volunteer to answer the question because

- usually the same few women volunteer;

- waiting for volunteers consumes time, causing the discussion to drag.

This is also your greatest tool for maintaining control! You can bring out shy women while keeping talkers from dominating. Call on the quiet women early in the discussion because often when they have participated and been affirmed, they find it easier to speak up. If you prefer not to call on women by name, do your best to give everyone an opportunity to participate.

Move quickly through questions with obvious answers. For example, observation questions can be answered easily right from the text. Call on one person and then move on, or quickly answer the question yourself as a transition to other kinds of questions.

Spend most of the discussion time on sharing and opinion questions. Sharing and opinion questions bring out interesting discussion. Your ultimate goal is to encourage natural interaction. As the women become more comfortable, you'll see a more natural interchange, with women speaking up in response to one another. This makes the group less like a question and answer schoolroom session. That's good!

This type of discussion, however, takes more skill to control. If the group becomes chaotic and the quieter ones are not participating, step back in and take control. Otherwise, let this more natural interaction continue—but learn to sum up ideas expressed and move on to the next question when appropriate. You are responsible for the flow of discussion.

7. Use Volunteers for Share Questions

Let the women know that personal application questions are for *volunteers only!* It's inappropriate to ask a woman to reveal personal information unless she's ready. Our goal, however, is to share our heartaches and struggles. How can you facilitate a deep level of personal sharing? *Be ready to share occasionally on personal application questions.* Be real with the group! A great benefit of discussion groups is that we build community when participants open up about their fears or feelings of inadequacy. Guard, though, against spending too much time working through personal problems. Life's answers are found in Scripture.

8. Be Sure Every Comment Is Affirmed!

The leader must be sure every comment is acknowledged in a positive way. Nothing feels more awkward than to express an idea and have it ignored. This conveys rejection. If no one else in the group interacts or responds to the comment, then the leader must affirm the group member with warm words like, "Thank you for your insight," or at least, "That's an interesting way of looking at it." Try to respond as you would in everyday conversation, as naturally as possible. *Affirming the women is a necessity!*

Quick affirmations besides "good point" are

Excellent	Fantastic
Super	Great answer
Wonderful	Terrific

Wow	Fabulous
Absolutely	I agree
What insight	That was deep
I like that	Wish I had thought of that

Among group affirmations are

- "I'm so happy to see all of you!"

- "There are many places you could be today, and I'm so glad you chose to be here!"

- "Thank you for being so well prepared."

- "I appreciate each one of you and the effort you made to be here."

9. Keep Up the Pace

The pace of the discussion is determined by the personalities of the group members and the skill and preparation of the leader. Observe the pace of your group. Is it peppy or does it drag? Develop strategies to keep the group moving and interesting. There are two extremes, and each requires a different response.

A. *The quiet group.* Does your group hesitate to answer? Do you feel like you are "pulling teeth" to get them to participate? Then you have a quiet group. They often water-ski over issues and are content with pat answers. Their pace is too slow—it drags—and they tend to finish quickly. But when the discussion is over, it wasn't very interesting. What can you do to perk up a quiet group and shoot it full of energy?

- Muster enthusiasm.

- Encourage, encourage, encourage.

- Be patient; intimacy takes time.

- Ask energetic women to interject stimulating questions to spark interest.

- Draw out answers by calling on many women for each question.

- Don't settle for a pat answer.

B. *The talkative group.* This group has difficulty finishing the questions because so many women want to participate. The pace is perky and fun, but the discussion is easily sidetracked. When you go down rabbit trails, you talk about issues unrelated to the Bible study. This is frustrating for women who want to understand and apply the passage. When you seldom finish the lesson, the more serious students become discouraged.

The group is filled with women who love to talk and have interesting ideas to contribute. The problem comes when the more verbal women dominate those who are less articulate, and when the group can't get through the lesson. What can you do?

- Assume a greater air of authority.

- Privately elicit the more talkative women's help in drawing out quieter women.

- Cut off talkers (as graciously as possible).

To refocus a group, here are some things you could say:

- "In the interest of our time remaining, let's move on."

- "Let's pick up the pace a little."

- "Let's finish that discussion after Bible study."

- "Let's finish our questions, and then we'll come back to this."

Whenever the group is sidetracked, the leader must decide how much time she'll spend there. Pursue a rabbit trail *briefly* if it's of common interest and time allows. Then get back to the meat of the lesson. Do your utmost to finish every week. The women expect it!

What should you do if a woman breaks down in tears? This *special circumstance* can stall the pace and tempt the group to get sidetracked for the rest of the lesson. *DON'T!*

Be sensitive, but also think of the group as a whole. The group often wants to spend the remaining time consoling, counseling, and fixing the problem. You can't! Allow a couple minutes of tender feedback, but then step in and *pray briefly* for the woman. Assure her you will talk with her later. Then move on. Later, talk with her privately and give her your encouragement and support. But *do not discontinue working through the lesson.*

10. Control Your Own Talking

The leader is in ministry to others. This is the participants' time! If the group is a talkative group, the leader should limit her talking. If the group tends to be a quiet group, talk to prime the pump and then back off when the women are participating.

11. Maintain Unity of Spirit

Never speak in a critical manner about any church or denomination, and do your best to discourage this kind of talking in the group. A woman may be offended if another group member slanders a group the woman grew up in or respects. Avoid politics. Redirect the conversation. This kind of talk is divisive, destroying the unity we are striving to build.

12. Stay in Touch with Your Group

Keep in touch regularly with your group—by phone or e-mail. If you never contact them, you're sending them a message that you don't care! Let them know that you're praying for them—especially if they're absent. This builds relationships. If a new member joins the group, be sure to call the first week to answer any questions and familiarize her with group procedures. You are a shepherdess—so tenderly nurture your flock.

Will Your Group Pray Together?

If so, here are suggested methods:

- Let the women know that there will be prayer time and ask them to submit a *personal* request.

- Encourage the women to write out their requests as they do their lesson rather than waiting to do so until they arrive.

- Ask your group to write down their prayer requests on 3 x 5 index cards.

- Collect the cards and *you* (the leader) read the requests aloud to the group. Share any answered prayer at this time.

- Either pass the cards back out to the group or place them in the middle.

- Ask the group members each to pick a card and pray for the request during the group prayer time or during the week.

- As the leader is reading the requests, the women can write them down, or one person can keep a group prayer journal.

- A volunteer can e-mail the requests to group members.

Leader's Guide

BEFORE YOU BEGIN . . .

I'm delighted that you've decided to lead a group through *Daddy's Girls: Discover the Wonder of the Father*. Familiarize yourself with this overview as preparation for inviting women to join you.

Daddy's Girls transforms lives! Ask women who are interested in attending this question: *Which of these statements best reflects your relationship with your earthly father when you were a little girl—"Daddy is really proud of me" or "Daddy is really mad at me"?* The way a woman answers has profound impact on her relationship with God as well as how she views herself as a woman. It also affects the men she is attracted to and the way she relates to males in her home, workplace, church, and community.

Explain to potential participants that throughout the study, they will compare their relationships with their earthly fathers to their relationships with their heavenly Father. Earthly fathers come in all shapes and sizes, but no matter whether they were strong and supportive, disengaged, or abusive, they were our first loves.

In previous *Daddy's Girls* group studies, I discovered that only about a quarter of the women described their earthly dad as "a good father." These dads were dependable, involved, and interested over the course of their daughters' lives. Most of these women said they grew up reasonably confident, free of crippling self-doubt, and comfortable in the company of men. But these were unusual fathers. More women used words like passive, absent, distant, demanding, and a few even used the word seductive. As a result, many of these women struggled to see their heavenly Father as He really is. The women who join you will have different kinds of dads too, requiring you to lead with sensitivity to their unique situations.

As you invite women, stress that the questions are designed to lead them into a clearer understanding of God as their heavenly Father, not to focus on ways their earthly dads messed up. Understanding our earthly dads is important, but knowing God as our forever heavenly Father is the priority. Regardless of her dad's imprint on her life, any woman can become a Daddy's Girl.

No Father Bashing

Whatever words women use to describe their earthly fathers, remind them that no father is perfect and we are all sinners. Tell the women that you won't waste valuable group time bashing fathers. It's counterproductive and unacceptable. Please don't misunderstand—understanding earthly fathers is important, expanding our awareness of their impact on us, but the majority of this work will be done in private, in the home study.

Women Who Resist

When we invited women to join us, most women were enthusiastic. We were surprised, however, at the reactions from a few—women who told us they were afraid to delve into aspects of their painful relationships with their earthly fathers. Some were estranged from their fathers. Others had buried unresolved issues in relationships with their dads. And some carried on seemingly normal relationships, yet deep wounds continued to harass them. Whatever the situation, they all echoed a similar refrain: "I'm terrified that this study will hurt too much."

You may encounter similar women. Explain that a refusal to do business with their earthly father is probably hindering their relationship with God the Father. Encourage these women to lay aside their fears and to trust God to use this study to heal these dysfunctional relationships or at least enable them to move forward in their spiritual lives. Remind them that healing comes when we bring our wounds into the light. We found that with reassurance, and occasionally a bit of positive pressure, most of these women signed up. Their courage paid powerful dividends by the end of the study! Almost all voiced hearty gratitude that we had encouraged them to face their fears. Boldly speak into the lives of hurting women for their ultimate good!

Resource

To listen to an introductory lecture by the author, go to http://www.irvingbible.org/index .php?id=133, and select *Daddy's Girls*, then "Father Hunger: Taste and See that the Lord Is Good."

LESSON 1: WITHIN THE TRANSCENDENT GOD BEATS A FATHER'S HEART

Getting Acquainted

Open with prayer. Should you pray or invite one of the participants to do so? Be sensitive to the women. If they are comfortable praying out loud, give them opportunity. If not, you, as the leader, pray. Then spend time getting to know one another. You might, for example, ask each woman to introduce herself by telling something about family, hobbies, what she likes to do on a Saturday night, a pet peeve, or what she hopes to gain from the study. If time allows, spend your first meeting connecting with each other, using questions or icebreaker games. For an extended community builder, ask that each participant bring a significant object in her life (picture, keepsake, artifact) and explain why it's significant.

An Optional Weekly Connecting Activity

Ask each woman to provide a photograph of herself as a little girl with her dad. Show one or two pictures at the beginning of each study, as time allows. If you're in a large study setting, project the picture on a screen as the women enter. If you're meeting in a more intimate setting, pass the picture around. Try to guess which women are the little girls in the pictures.

If desired, the participant can take a few minutes to tell an interesting story about her dad and their relationship. I suggest you give her a time limit, maybe three to five minutes, and ask her to write out what she plans to say. Review it with her and stress the importance of honoring the time limit. Also, do not pressure women to participate. Women with painful pasts won't want to be involved. This activity works best in a large group where no one feels singled out if they don't join in.

Getting Focused

Look over the study guide with the group and express your excitement about the topic. Discuss group ground rules. If women join you later, remember to orient them, too. Stress the importance of confidentiality.

Some women come to Bible study with the sole purpose of studying Scripture. Others come for community, to find friends. Regardless of your own bent, honor both desires. We all need a relationship with God through serious Bible study *and* relationships with other women through connecting in authentic community. Ensure the schedule provides time to dig deep into God's Word and to build relationships.

Discuss Lesson 1

To enhance your small-group leading skills, study the "Training Guide for Small-Group Leaders" on pages 74–79 until you are familiar with its concepts. Remember that leading a small group is a complex skill, requiring lots of practice. Be patient and reread the Training Guide often.

Did you ask women to come prepared to discuss the first lesson? If so, begin by quickly summarizing the introductory page to focus their minds to the day's topic. Guide the group through the study by reading the questions and drawing the women into discussion and discovery. Your role, as leader, is *not* to illumine the group with your answers but to provide a safe place for them to share what God is teaching them. Set an atmosphere in which they can respectfully explore different ideas without offending one another. Roadblocks to spiritual maturity become dismantled in these kinds of groups.

Don't expect deep sharing for the first few weeks. Women on occasion do bond quickly, but often they need time to develop trust in one another. If you can't cover all the questions each time you meet, plan ahead. Choose blocks of questions to cover as time allows and eliminate others. Or skim over observation questions and spend time on the opinion and application questions.

Content of Lesson 1

None of us chose our earthly fathers, but we can choose our heavenly Father—and He alone is a perfect Father. No matter our experience as little girls, we can experience the wonder of the heavenly Father. What is He like? Each lesson unfolds another divine attribute, contrasting God's characteristics with qualities lacking in many earthly fathers.

Lesson 1 contrasts two mysterious attributes of God the Father. He is transcendent—above and beyond all we can imagine or know. At the same time, He knows us intimately and involves Himself in every detail of our lives. His transcendence reflects His power, and His intimate knowledge of us reflects His unconditional love. Help women rest in this unfathomable mystery, and delight in these truths. As we will see later, His strength *and* His tenderness make Him the Father we need.

Creative Arts Ideas

- Play a film clip featuring dads and daughters.

- This lesson depicts God as a Father who earnestly desires to make contact with His daughters. Play a clip from the film *Contact* to introduce the concept.[1]

Resource

To hear a lecture on this lesson by the author, go to the following site and select *Daddy's Girls*, "Session One" at http://www.irvingbible.org/index.php?id=133.

LESSON 2: ABBA

Lesson Purpose

As little girls, we expected our earthly fathers to be perfect. In time, we learned they were only human. If our dads lacked integrity, wisdom, or stability, we struggled to respect them. Lesson 2 explores unrealistic expectations, with an eye to beginning the process of forgiveness. And we learn that our heavenly Father is always worthy of honor and respect, because He alone is holy, thus deserving of our worship.

Create a Positive Group Ethos

Ethos (*e-thas*) is the distinguishing environment or atmosphere of a place. As the leader you set the ethos, and although you cannot see it, women respond or shut down in response. Every home has ethos. In some homes children experience unconditional love and fair discipline. As a result they usually grow up confident and secure. Other homes exude a chill—children walk on eggshells, knowing that affection is earned by performance, and is easily withdrawn when they mess up.

Ethos has an impact in classrooms. In some classes, you're comfortable asking questions, even dumb ones. You know the teacher won't intentionally embarrass you and has your best interest at heart. In others, you don't dare open your mouth. Why? Ethos.

The women who walk into your small group will be influenced by ethos. Will your group be a place where women can voice their deep hurts and difficult questions? Can women be honest and do business with God in your group? Only then can the process of forgiveness and healing take root. To learn how to create positive group ethos, review the "Training Guide for Small-Group Leaders," focusing on the importance of affirmation and controlling your own talking. Remember, the group time is not about you! It's about giving participants a safe place to discuss what *they* learned, try out *their* new ideas, and articulate *their* convictions.

Troubleshooting

Question 1 (page 22). During the study, women asked me, "Is God male like my dad?" Numbers 23:19 says that "God is not a man . . ." This verse and others reveal that God the Father is beyond gender. He is neither masculine nor feminine in His essence, although we observe both images in Scripture. This truth negates the popular idea espoused by some feminists that God is female—a mother figure or goddess. Jesus told the woman at the well, "God is spirit, and his worshipers must worship in spirit and in truth" (John 4:24). This truth helps women with memories of distant or abusive earthly fathers see God with new eyes. Viewing God the Father as spirit frees them from unbearable mind's eye pictures and allows them to worship Him anew.

Creative Arts Idea: Illustrate God's Holiness

(You'll need a clear pitcher, a basin of water, cups, and a food-color tablet.)

When we reach a particular age, our doctors usually instruct us to get a mammogram. The first test is called a baseline, used as a comparison to future tests. The baseline, then, colors how subsequent tests are seen. God's holiness is His baseline, coloring all His other attributes. Let's assume this pitcher is God and each of these cups represents one of His attributes. Pour in His love, next His forgiveness, His justice, His compassion, now His wrath. *(Pour in a cup of water as you mention each attribute.)*

This is God's holiness. *(Hold up the food-color tablet. Drop it in and stir.)* God's holiness colors every one of His attributes. When He pours out His compassion, it is holy compassion. When He pours out His love, it is holy love. When He pours out His justice, it is holy justice. Nor can one attribute be separated from the others, because they are all holy! Holiness is the essence of our Father, and our baseline for understanding that He alone is a Father worthy of honor.

Resource

Tozer, A. W. *The Knowledge of the Holy.* New York: Harper & Row, 1961.

LESSON 3: A FATHER WHO CHERISHES ME

For some women, God's love sounds like a cliché, difficult for them to grasp. After discussing the lesson, teach Zephaniah 3:17: "The LORD your God is with you . . . he will take great delight in you, he will quiet you with his love, he will rejoice over you with singing." Explain this passage line by line to help women fathom God's amazing love. Use stories below or find your own. Emphasize these truths:

- *Your Father delights in you!* Kathleen Norris tells the story of a young couple with an infant at an airport departure gate. Whenever the baby recognized a human face, no matter if it was young or old, pretty or ugly, bored or happy, she would erupt with delight. She writes, "It turned our drab gate into the gate of heaven."[2] Find stories that express love that delights.

- *Your Father quiets you with His love.* Once when we were babysitting our five-month-old granddaughter, she cried uncontrollably. We tried everything to calm her until finally we sent for her parents. As soon as her daddy took her in his arms, she collapsed limp like a rag doll. He quieted her with his love.

- *Your Father rejoices over you with singing.* We concluded our women's leadership training in Moscow with a celebration. Two of my students joined me, one sitting in front of me and the other behind me. One sang softly into my ear in Russian while the other translated behind me—a beautiful song of gratitude and love. I wept. The Hebrew word for rejoice suggests "dancing for joy"—spinning around with intense motion. Picture God, your Father, spinning around you! The God of the universe sings and dances over you, His daughter. Dr. Ian Pitt-Watson said, "Some things are loved because they are worthy; some things are worthy because they are loved."[3] Help your group understand they are worthy because they are loved.

Troubleshooting

Question block 4–9 (pages 33–36). Psalm 107 identifies different people groups that God rescued, expressing His loving kindness. The four groups represent homeless, searching wanderers (5.1), rebellious people in bondage (6.1), distressed and depressed people (7.1), and impulsive adventurers (8.1). Help women see themselves in one or more of these groups. Point out how God treats them when they fail or grieve Him.

Creative Arts Ideas

- Display pictures of forlorn, fatherless children and Psalm 68:4 and 5, "Sing to God, sing praise to his name, extol him who rides on the clouds—his name is the LORD—and rejoice before him. A Father to the fatherless."

- Create a book mark or magnet with the words of Zephaniah 3:17.

- Isaiah 49:16 says, "I have engraved you on the palms of my hands." Provide washable colored markers for the women to write Zephaniah 3:17 on their hands, reminding them all day of God's unfailing love.

- Follow the discussion and teaching with worship or prayer, thanking God for His love expressed in Zephaniah 3:17.

Resource

Brumberg, Joan Jacobs. *The Body Project*. New York: Vintage Books, 1997.

LESSON 4: A FATHER I CAN COUNT ON!

Lesson Purpose

Remind the group that in lesson 3 they explored God's amazing love. To thrive as Daddy's Girls, however, they also need to know that He is able to help them—we need a Father's love *and* strength. This lesson focuses on four important theological truths about the nature of God's abilities:

- God is omnipresent—He is everywhere at once.

- God is omniscient—He knows about everything, including us: our past, present, and future.

- God is omnipotent—He is all powerful, able to do whatever He wills.

- God is immutable—He does not change.

To become secure and confident, they must grasp these truths about their heavenly Father. In this lesson, they will discover a Father who is powerful enough to act on their behalves, who knows enough to act wisely, and who never changes. He is a Father they can count on.

Troubleshooting

As women explore God's abilities, they often ask why God allows bad things to happen to good people. Welcome the question and assure them that it will be addressed in lesson 5.

Toss the Rabbit

This lesson is full of share and opinion questions. Mark them on your lesson to help you identify them. I put a big pink heart next to each share question to distinguish them from other kinds of questions. Remember that share questions are for volunteers only.

Participants tend to go down rabbit trails on share and opinion questions. Follow the trail if you discern the discussion is interesting and is bonding the group. But watch your time—don't allow the group to wander too far.

One technique to curb rabbit trails is called "Toss the Rabbit." Consider purchasing an inexpensive little plastic or stuffed rabbit and explain its purpose to the group. Set the rabbit within reach, and when you, or a participant, sense it is time to get back on track, toss the rabbit into the middle of the group. It's good for a laugh but also serves as a cue that everyone understands. It's time to move on!

Optional Prayer Time Activity

Question 5 (page 45) asks women to list problems in their lives that seem impossible and then asks how *they* would solve these problems. Next, they are challenged to submit these problems to God to solve *His* way. Use question 5 as the basis for your prayer time. Consider asking a volunteer to record willing women's lists in the group's prayer journal. Periodically check to see how God is answering these prayers with either "yes," "no," or "wait." Discuss what you learn.

Resource

Packer, J. I. *Knowing God.* Downers Grove, IL: InterVarsity, 1993.

LESSON 5: "FATHER KNOWS BEST"

Troubleshooting

Wrestling with concepts like God's sovereignty, election, free will, and human responsibility is challenging, making this lesson the most difficult in the study. As you begin the discussion, lay some ground rules. Alert participants that the topic is difficult and people hold divergent views. Remind them to listen respectfully to each other's ideas even if they disagree.

Consider preparing a short teaching time at the end to crystallize concepts in the lesson. You may want to present some of the different views, reminding the women that brilliant scholars disagree. The extensive note at the end of the lesson should help you. Read and digest it carefully. During the discussion, though, you probably won't answer related questions to everyone's satisfaction. If respected scholars disagree—and they do—don't expect to nail down these mysteries. Theologians attempt, nevertheless, to give us insight that you may want to present at the end. Remember that your role during the discussion is to lead—not lecture. Let the participants wrestle with what they think during the discussion. Then, if you chose to present a wrap-up message after the discussion, exchange your leader's hat for a teacher's hat.

In addition to the extensive note at the end of the lesson, here are some ideas to consider. God did not create us as robots, forced to follow and love Him, because He cannot enjoy a meaningful relationship with a robot. Love and discipleship cannot be forced. They must be chosen—which requires free will. The down side of free will is that sometimes we choose not to love or follow God. And sometimes we choose to sin, hurting not only ourselves but others. Genesis 3 reveals that in this fallen world, sin breeds sadness, sickness, and death. As a result, bad things happen to good people.

But God grieves with us over this state of affairs. He is in the process of redeeming and restoring the earth. When we struggle and suffer, God knows, cares, and helps if we ask. Our pain also enables us to comfort others. Remember that these troubles are temporary—a far better eternity waits. As women understand these biblical truths, they can reframe their perspective when life seems unfair, full of heartache and trials. Help women in the group surface some of these ideas as they discuss the lesson.

You may want to explain that the sovereignty of God and free will is called an antinomy—two truths that seem contradictory, yet both are undeniable. God's Word contains solid evidence for both. J. I. Packer insists, "We must teach ourselves to think in a way that provides for the peaceful co-existence of these truths, because reality has proven to contain them both."[4] Therefore we are wise to live within this tension, resting on God's declaration that both are true even if we can't completely unravel the mystery.

Women on occasion bring up related theological views—for example, Calvinism and Armenianism. Five point Calvinism emphasizes God's sovereignty and discounts free will. Armenianism overemphasizes free choice and discounts God's sovereignty. You may have women in the group that subscribe to one of these views. Remind them to present their ideas gently, and encourage others to listen respectfully. For further study, refer them to the "Resources."

Question 6.2 (page 52). This question refers to a line in Peter's speech to the Jews at Pentecost. In the same verse (Acts 2:23), we observe both the sovereignty of God *and* the fact that men are held responsible for their choices. Peter declares that Jesus was handed over to the Jews to be crucified as part of God's sovereign plan. Peter goes on, however, calling the Jews "wicked men," holding them accountable for their part in what they did to Jesus. God's sovereign plan and man's free will are woven together *in the same verse!*

Resources

Packer, J. I. *Evangelism and the Sovereignty of God.* Downers Grove, IL: InterVarsity, 1991.

Sproul, R. C., Jr. *Almighty over All: Understanding the Sovereignty of God.* Grand Rapids: Baker, 1999.

LESSON 6: MY "JEALOUS" FATHER

Lesson Purpose

God is "jealous"? Usually the term denotes envy or resentment—not a term we use to describe a holy, righteous Father. In Exodus 34:14, however, the Jews were told, "Do not worship any other god, for the LORD, whose name is Jealous, is a jealous God." Unlike the jealousy of warped husbands or foolish boyfriends, God's jealousy is His zeal to preserve something or someone precious. Human jealousy is often self-focused and destructive whereas our Heavenly Father's jealousy is protective and constructive. Help the participants understand God's jealousy as a holy attribute, ultimately for their good.

Troubleshooting

Question 3 (pages 57–59) and the "Digging Deeper" question on page 60 delve into Old Testament parables—figurative language painting pictures of God's relationship with Israel. As we dissect these parables, we extract principles for today. If the group members are confused by these parables, help them understand that the Bible is composed of many kinds of literature. To interpret the Bible correctly, first we must discern what kind of literature we're studying. Then we work hard to understand and apply the message to our lives today.

The Bible contains narratives, biography, songs, poetry, parables, proverbs and wisdom literature, prophecy and apocalyptic literature, exposition, letters, and speeches. *Living by the Book* by Howard Hendricks and William Hendricks is an invaluable resource, teaching us how to observe, interpret, apply, and correlate the Scripture references with skill and accuracy.[5] I highly recommend this book.

In this lesson, Ezekiel weaves stories illustrating God's righteous jealousy toward a wayward daughter and wife. These women represent unfaithful Israel who are worshipping pagan gods and goddesses like Baal, Asherah, and Artemis. Sometimes the Jews did not completely abandon God for these false gods and goddesses. Instead they worshipped both. But God was not willing to share one ounce of His glory. He alone has every right to demand complete devotion from His children, true today as it was then.

In vivid language, we observe God as a passionate protective Father, grieved and angered by these women's actions and attitudes. Guide the group members to apply ways they may be unfaithful to God. They may not worship graven images, but do they ask God to share His glory with something or someone else? God's jealousy is like appropriate jealousy of a husband for his wife. Who would criticize a man for wanting his wife to be fully devoted to him, not to chase after other men or spend excessive amounts of time thinking or lusting after them? The Bible says that Christians are the Bride of Christ. He demands single-minded devotion!

An idol is anything that occupies our thoughts, time, effort, and energy to the exclusion of God. What competes for our devotion to our heavenly Father? A designer outfit, a new sofa, the latest hairstyle, our work, our family, another person? Idols come in all shapes and sizes. Help the women identify less obvious idols that may be replacing or supplementing their devotion to God. For aid in understanding particular parts of the stories, refer to *The Bible Knowledge Commentary: An Exposition of the Scriptures, Old Testament*.[6] This book comes as a two-volume set, Old and New Testament, offering help from expert scholars, written without complicated jargon.[7]

Creative Arts Ideas

- Play a *Gone with the Wind* clip showing Scarlet's jealousy of Melanie's relationship with Ashley.

- Display "Five Simple Rules for Dating My Daughter" to jump-start discussion:

Rule 1:   If you pull into my driveway and honk, you'd better be delivering a package, because you're sure not picking anything up.

Rule 2:   You do not touch my daughter in front of me. You may glance at her, so long as you do not peer at anything below her neck. If you cannot keep your eyes or hands off my daughter's body, I will remove them.

Rule 3:   I am aware that it is considered fashionable for boys of your age to wear their trousers so loosely that they appear to be falling off their hips. Please don't take this as an insult, but you and your friends are complete idiots. Still, I want to be fair and open minded about this issue, so I propose a compromise. You may come to the door with your underwear showing and your pants ten sizes too big; however, in order to ensure that your clothes do not, in fact, come off during your date with my daughter, I will take my electric nail gun and fasten your trousers securely to your waist.

Rule 4:   I am sure you have been told that, in today's world, sex without utilizing a "barrier method" of some kind will kill you. Let me elaborate. When it comes to sex, I am the barrier, and I will kill you.

Rule 5:   Do not lie to me. I may appear to be a potbellied, balding, middle-aged, dim-witted has-been. But on issues relating to my daughter, I am the all-knowing, merciless god of the universe. Do not trifle with me!

Resources

Dallas Seminary Faculty. *The Bible Knowledge Commentary: An Exposition of the Scriptures, New Testament.* Edited by John F. Walvoord and Roy B. Zuck. Wheaton, IL: Victor Books, 1983.

————. *The Bible Knowledge Commentary: An Exposition of the Scriptures, Old Testament.* Edited by John F. Walvoord and Roy B. Zuck. Wheaton, IL: Victor Books, 1985.

Hendricks, Howard G., and William D. Hendricks. *Living by the Book.* Chicago: Moody, 1991.

LESSON 7: A FATHER WHO IS FAIR

Troubleshooting

This lesson, like lesson 5 on God's sovereignty and man's responsibility, may raise questions. We expect justice, but we learn, in time, that life is unfair. God declares that He loves justice, yet injustice is rampant. Your group may ask, "How do we reconcile these realities?"

Consider teaching a wrap-up message to clarify this tension and provide biblical answers. An outline for your message might include these principles:

- God is not the cause of earthly injustice (Gen. 3).

- God is withholding His justice (2 Peter 3:3–10).

- One day God will ride with justice (Rev. 19:11–15).

- God gives us a glimmer of justice now (examples of God's justice).

This lesson reveals God's plan to destroy the earth and replace it with a new heaven and a new earth. The culmination of time and life as we know it may frighten members of your group. Help them see that God is in the process of restoring the world to its original beauty, providing a perfect home to share with us, His daughters.

This lesson (particularly question 3, pages 65–66) assumes a premillennial, pretribulation view of the end times—a literal interpretation of Revelation based on the rapture of Christians before a seven-year tribulation and the establishment of Christ's thousand-year kingdom upon the earth before the new heaven the new earth. If you, or women in your group, hold a different end times view, use this lesson to better understand the premillennial, pretribulation view. For more insight into this view, see J. Dwight Pentecost's *Things to Come*.[8] Stress the importance of discussing end times perspectives with grace and respect.

Invite Women to Become a Daddy's Girl

You have spent many hours together in this study developing a relationship. Are there women in your small group who may not be Christians? Pray that God will identify these women, help you discern their readiness, and, if they are ready, show you how to encourage them toward a relationship with Jesus.

Question 5 (page 68) is included to invite them into God's family. The question asks the women to look up several verses that explain God's plan of salvation. Other passages clarifying the gospel are John 5:24; Romans 3:23; 6:23; 1 Corinthians 15:3–5 (the gospel in a nutshell); and Ephesians 2:8–9. Familiarize yourself with these verses in preparation. Ask the Holy Spirit to guide your words and enable you to know what to say and when to say it. You may want to discuss how to become a Christian with the whole group and then challenge women to make a decision on their own or with you later. Tell them you would love to talk privately to anyone who would like to discuss salvation further. Use discretion and wisdom, remembering salvation is the Spirit's work. He may, however, desire to use you as His instrument.

Creative Arts Idea

Locate Peanuts cartoon by Charles Schulz for Sunday, April 7, 2002, when the little blonde-headed girl rails against the injustice of a "C" on her coat-hanger sculpture. Display and use to prime the pump.

Resources

Pentecost, J. Dwight. *Things to Come: A Study in Biblical Eschatology*. Grand Rapids: Zondervan, 1958.

Strauss, Richard L. *The Joy of Knowing God*. Neptune, NJ: Loizeaux Brothers, 1984.

LESSON 8: "HERE IS YOUR GOD"

Lesson Purpose

Lesson 8's purpose is twofold. The first question asks participants to study Isaiah 40, matching verses with our heavenly Father's attributes. This amazing passage contains multiple descriptions of God the Father, serving to summarize the entire study. As you lead this section of the lesson, don't let women skim over the question. You may want to read the passage aloud or display it in some fashion before you begin. The second question, "Rediscover Your Father," asks hard questions relating to women's relationships with their earthly fathers. You may want to use these questions for the participants' personal reflection only. For many groups, these issues are painful, best suited for a private setting. Certainly, if you discuss them in the group, ask for volunteers. If you determine that discussing these questions would be beneficial for your particular group, I suggest that you do not read questions 2.1–11 (pages 71–73). Simply ask if anyone wants to share about anything she's learned concerning her relationship with her earthly father.

However you decide to handle the personal questions, ask question 2.12 (page 73). This multiple-part question contains wrap-up questions to help the group reflect on what they've learned and where they go from here.

Saying Good-bye or Going On Together?

Is this a short-term group, or do you, as the leader, want to continue meeting? The first decision is yours. Count the cost. Is the group thriving? Bonding? Committed? Worth the effort you're investing? Answer these questions honestly. Every group has a beginning and an end. Is this the time for your group to disband? If so, tell the group your reasons, kindly but emphatically. Don't be pressured into continuing against your better judgment.

If you determine you're excited about leading the group through another study, you may want to poll the group to learn their desires. If so, plan a date to meet for a brainstorming session on what to study and what changes might be in order, if any.

Either way, use this last gathering of *Daddy's Girls* to reflect, review, and celebrate what has been accomplished. Plan a time that fosters a sense of closure for this particular study, possibly festive food, a potluck brunch or luncheon, or some other special activity. An example of an activity might be writing a psalm of praise, listing benefits in the lives of women as a result of the study. Share changes you observed in the members as a result of sharing this study. In some way, celebrate this final chapter in your group experience. Praise and thank God for what He has done in your lives individually and as a worshipping community. If any of the participants are leaving the group, be sure to say good-bye and pray for them.

Creative Arts Idea

Secure a copy of Dennis Rainey's book *The Tribute*.[9] From his book, explain to participants what it means, and does not mean, to honor your parents. He suggests writing a formal tribute, a document possibly typeset or in calligraphy, matted and framed that expresses appreciation to earthly parents. Creating this document often helps children work through issues and focus on the positives, putting to rest some matters that have plagued them and hindered them from moving forward spiritually. Provide a copy of Dennis's tribute to his mother as an example should any group members decide to tackle this project. Familiarize women with the concept but don't pressure them or make this a "have-to" project. Victims of abuse need to be under the care of a professional counselor before deciding whether to continue a relationship with abusive parents. Refer them. This project is appropriate for many women, however, and may serve as a fitting way to overcome painful memories and move on.

Resource

Rainey, Dennis. *The Tribute: What Every Parent Longs to Hear.* Nashville: Nelson, 1994.

Notes

Lesson 1: Within the Transcendent God Beats a Father's Heart

1. Victoria Secunda, *Women and Their Fathers* (New York: Delacorte Press, 1992), front flap.

Lesson 2: Abba

1. A. W. Tozer, *The Knowledge of the Holy* (1961; repr., San Francisco: HarperSanFrancisco, 1992), 166–67.

Lesson 3: A Father Who Cherishes Me

1. Victoria Secunda, *Women and Their Fathers* (New York: Delacorte Press, 1992), 221.
2. Ibid., 287.

Lesson 4: A Father I Can Count On!

1. Victoria Secunda, *Women and Their Fathers* (New York: Delacorte Press, 1992), 79.
2. Ibid., 193.
3. Richard L. Strauss, *The Joy of Knowing God* (Neptune, NJ: Loizeaux Brothers, 1984), 77.
4. Secunda, *Women and Their Fathers*, 3.
5. Quoted in Arthur W. Pink, *The Attributes of God* (Grand Rapids: Baker, 1975), 47.
6. Secunda, *Women and Their Fathers*, 378.
7. Pink, *Attributes of God*, 51.

Lesson 5: "Father Knows Best"

1. Victoria Secunda, *Women and Their Fathers* (New York: Delacorte Press, 1992), 147–48.
2. Ibid.
3. Louis Berkhof, *Systematic Theology* (Grand Rapids: Eerdmans, 1938), 66.

Lesson 6: My "Jealous" Father

1. Victoria Secunda, *Women and Their Fathers* (New York: Delacorte Press, 1992), 104.
2. Ibid., 312.
3. J. I. Packer, *Knowing God* (Downers Grove, IL: InterVarsity, 1973), 153.

Lesson 7: A Father Who Is Fair

1. Victoria Secunda, *Women and Their Fathers* (New York: Delacorte Press, 1992), 153.

Lesson 8: "Here Is Your God"

1. Victoria Secunda, *Women and Their Fathers* (New York: Delacorte Press, 1992), 359.

Leader's Guide

1. *Contact*, with Jodie Foster and Matthew McConaughey (Warner Brothers, 1997), rating PG.

2. Kathleen Norris, quoted in Philip Yancey, *Reaching for the Invisible God* (Grand Rapids: Zondervan, 2002), 166.

3. Ian Pitt-Watson, quoted in Yancey, *Reaching for the Invisible God*, 165.

4. J. I. Packer, *Evangelism and the Sovereignty of God* (Downers Grove, IL: InterVarsity, 1991), 21.

5. Howard G. Hendricks and William D. Hendricks, *Living by the Book* (Chicago: Moody, 1991).

6. Dallas Seminary Faculty, *The Bible Knowledge Commentary: An Exposition of the Scriptures, Old Testament*, ed. John F. Walvoord and Roy B. Zuck (Wheaton, IL: Victor Books, 1983).

7. Dallas Seminary Faculty, *The Bible Knowledge Commentary: An Exposition of the Scriptures, Old Testament and New Testament*, ed. John F. Walvoord and Roy B. Zuck (Wheaton, IL: Victor Books, 1985).

8. J. Dwight Pentecost, *Things to Come: A Study in Biblical Eschatology* (Grand Rapids: Zondervan, 1958).

9. Dennis Rainey, *The Tribute: What Every Parent Longs to Hear* (Nashville: Nelson, 1994).

About the Author

Sue Edwards is assistant professor of Christian education (her specialization is women's studies) at Dallas Theological Seminary where she has the opportunity to equip men and women for future ministry. She brings over thirty years of experience into the classroom as a Bible teacher, curriculum writer, and overseer of several megachurch women's ministries. As pastor to women at Irving Bible Church and director of women's ministry at Prestonwood Baptist Church in Dallas, she has worked with women from all walks of life, ages, and stages. Her passion is to see modern and postmodern women connect, learn from one another, and bond around God's Word. Her Bible studies have ushered thousands of women all over the country and overseas into deeper Scripture study and community experiences.

Sue is the author of *New Doors in Ministry to Women: A Fresh Model for Transforming Your Church, Campus, or Mission Field*, and *Women's Retreats: A Creative Planning Guide*. Kelley Mathews coauthored both books and is currently partnering with Sue and Henry Rogers on a book about men and women working as brothers and sisters in our oversexed society (scheduled to be released in 2008).

Sue has a doctor of ministry degree from Gordon-Conwell Theological Seminary in Boston and a master's in Bible from Dallas Theological Seminary. With Dr. Joye Baker, she will be overseeing a new Dallas Theological Seminary doctor of ministry degree in Christian education with a women-in-ministry emphasis, beginning summer 2008.

Sue has been married to David for thirty-five years. They have two married daughters, Heather and Rachel, and four grandchildren, Becca, Luke, Caleb, and Will. David is a CAD applications engineer, a lay prison chaplain, and founder of their church's prison ministry.

More Studies to Help You Grow

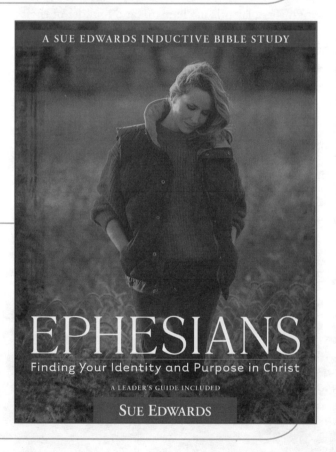

Discover the Wisdom of God

This insightful companion to Sue Edwards's inductive study of Proverbs explores more selections of ancient wisdom. In this nine-week study, Sue guides readers as they explore these timeless life lessons and apply them to our postmodern world.

978-0-8254-2548-6 • 96 pages • $11.99
Coming in October 2007!

Living a Victorious Christian Life

The church in Ephesus was surrounded by debauchery and occultism, yet Ephesian believers persevered as strong Christians. Using Paul's advice to this fledgling church, Sue shows readers how to stay strong in Christ in any situation through this nine-week Bible study.

978-0-8254-2549-3 • 96 pages • $11.99
Coming in October 2007!